Outfitting
Your Canoe or C-1

Charlie Walbridge

Illustrations by Grant Tatum

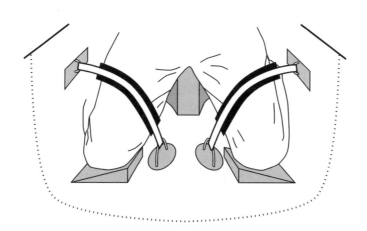

Menasha Ridge Press
Birmingham, Alabama

Printed in the United States of America
Published by Menasha Ridge Press
First edition, first printing

Illustrations by Grant Tatum
Text design by Carolina Graphics Group

Note: Outdoor activities are assumed risk sports. While every effort has been made to insure this book reflects current-practice boating skills and techniques, it is only a guide. It cannot be expected to replace an approved and appropriate course in kayaking, swimming or lifesavintg techniques.

Menasha Ridge Press
700 South 28th Street
Suite 206
Birmingham, Alabama 35233
(800) 247-9437

Contents

Introduction

Improperly placed fittings can be dangerous

Whitewater paddlers don't just sit inside a canoe; they wear them! Well designed, correctly placed outfitting is vital for safety and performance. A canoe should fit snugly and comfortably, like a good pair of athletic shoes, so you can transmit strokes and leans cleanly and quickly to your craft. A paddler must also be able to "punch out" of their boat quickly in an emergency. Improperly placed fittings can be uncomfortable, ineffective, or even dangerous!

Some canoeists believe that outfitting must be extremely tight for good performance. This is simply not true. You should use muscle power, not friction from outfitting, to hold yourself in place. Your fittings should never be so tight that they cut off blood circulation or cause pain. They should permit you to "ease off" the fittings in flat water or easy rapids for comfort, then "tighten up" above more serious drops for improved boat control.

Outfitting must never stand in the way of a fast exit. Excessively tight outfitting can trap you in a boat during emergencies with disastrous results. If you should "hang up" during a wet exit, consider it a warning to isolate the problem and fix it at once. You may not get another chance!

Whitewater boat outfitting has advanced considerably from the days when crudely formed parts were held in place with scraps of fiberglass. Many of today's canoes can be taken directly from the store to the water with minor adjustments, and numerous aftermarket outfitting kits are available to make your boat fit perfectly. An understanding of exactly how canoe paddlers hold themselves in their boats, coupled with a few shop skills, will allow you to do a good job.

As an active paddler I've spent a lot of time over the years outfitting whitewater boats for myself and my friends. I saw first hand how simple modifications can make a big difference. Later, as a canoe and kayak dealer, I spent countless hours showing people how to set up their boats for comfort, safety, and performance. Ironically, as the sport grows, specialty shops run by paddling enthusiasts are becoming less common (I closed my own business in 1995!). The paddlesport business will be increasingly dominated by large sporting goods chains. If their staff doesn't have this information, this little book will!

Not surprisingly, the folks at Dagger and Headwaters often field questions from customers on boat outfitting. They shared my desire to get this handbook into print. Frankie Hubbard from Ocoee Canoe and Headwaters and Mojo Rogers from Dagger provided considerable assistance in preparing this book. Thanks, guys!

See you on a river,

Charlie Walbridge

Outfitting Open Boats

How Canoe Outfitting Works

Whitewater canoeists kneel in their boats and use a single bladed paddle. Open canoes usually come from the factory with no outfitting installed, and most decked boats are inadequately equipped. Knee pads, made from Minicell, provide padding and support. Thigh straps crossing the upper leg at mid-thigh allow paddlers to hold onto the canoe by squeezing their legs together. Toe blocks are set so the paddler can push forward, into the straps, with their feet, eliminating the need for straps that are excessively tight or confining. But first, you must make sure the canoe is structurally sound.

Thwarts

Thwarts provide structural integrity to a boat

These rounded crossbars run from gunwale to gunwale across the top of an open canoe. They are vital to the boat's structural integrity and keep the hull from flattening and folding when pinned against a rock. The middle thwart is the most important, but whitewater canoes should have at least three thwarts, one near the center and the other two set about one-third of the way back from the bow and stern. Boats over 13' should be fitted with four thwarts; those over 15' with five. Not only do they provide structural integrity, they also help support canoe seats.

Thwarts are attached to the underside of the gunwale using stainless steel bolts, nuts and washers (on top and bottom). Normally one 1/4" bolt is used at each end, although if the inside of a wood gunwale is particularly narrow, two 1/8" bolts are better. To be sure that a thwart is not put in cockeyed, check to see that the distance from the

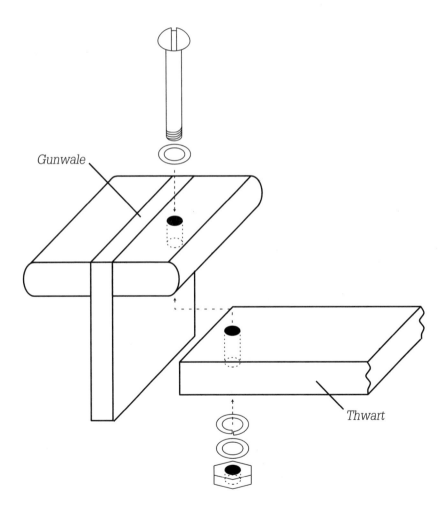

bow or stern to each end is identical. Clamp the thwart into place and drill the holes, being careful not to come too close to the canoe's hull or the edges of the gunwale. Tighten the bolts snugly. Lock washers next to the nut will keep the fittings tight. The bolt should be cut flush with the nut so it cannot cath on your body during a wet exit.

Flotation

By displacing water, flotation bags keep a swamped canoe light enough to manage. If the canoe swamps, the bags displace water, making the boat float higher. This makes it harder to pin, lighter and easier to rescue, and less likely to be damaged while floating through rapids.

C-1's use air bags shaped to fill the unoccupied bow and stern, leaving space for the paddler. Float bags are simply put on either side of the foam wall and inflated. They expand to fit your boat, and friction keeps them from working loose. Paddlers expecting violent big water swims can tie the ends of their float bags together in front of the foam walls. This is a lengthy job, requiring the removal and replacement of the front and rear walls. Most paddlers don't bother. If an air bag is too long, you can fold the end over and tape it to itself with duct tape.

Open boaters install triangular shaped flotation bags under the thwarts, with the narrow part pushed into the end of the canoe. These bags must be lashed down to keep them in place; when water enters a canoe, it gets under the float bags and tries to lift them up and out. While some open boaters like to install bags so long that there's no room left for anything but the paddler, I recommend leaving two

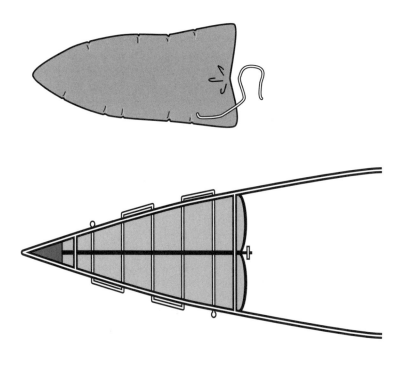

feet in front and behind the seat. This provides room
to bail, leaves a place to store gear; and makes the
boat considerably easier to roll.

The strongest and simplest way to install lashing is to drill a series of holes, 1/8" in diameter and 6
inches apart, underneath the gunwales. A 3 mm
lashing line running between the gunwales fills the
holes entirely and keeps the water out. If the thought
of drilling into your new canoe makes you cringe,
various fittings can be attached under the gunwales
to hold the lashing line securely.

Once the lashing is positioned, a keeper strap
made from 1" webbing should be installed. It runs
from the end plate to the center of the hull just behind
the wide part of the bag. How this strap is tied into

the end plate varies with the make and model of the canoe. If the plate is flimsy, a short "carrying thwart" can be installed underneath it to anchor the strap to serve as a carrying handle. The webbing now runs from the end plate, under the lashing lines and over the last one, and is attached to the hull with a D-Ring anchor.

The center bags used in tandem paddling are secured in the same way except that the keeper strap runs between two d-ring anchors set along the keel line at each end of the bag. Small "end" bags can be put in the bow of "end hole" boats. With "center cockpit" boats, solo floatation bags fill the spaces nicely. Anchors are discussed further in the thigh strap section.

Canoe Seats

While C-1's are usually outfitted with saddles, open boats have seats that come in many styles, ranging from the bench seats found in multipurpose craft to the kneeling thwarts, pedestals, and saddles used in whitewater boats.

The first thing to consider in a seat is height, measured from the bottom of the boat. As the seat is set lower, the occupant's center of gravity drops and the canoe becomes more stable. Many bench seats in lake canoes are positioned quite low to improve stability for seated paddlers. Whitewater paddlers kneel to lower their center of gravity further. If there is not enough clearance to tuck your feet underneath a low seat, you could become snagged upon capsizing with unpleasant results. The same danger may exist with low-slung kneeling thwarts.

Many elite slalom racers use seats less than 6

As a seat is set lower, the canoe becomes more stable.

inches high. This will be quite uncomfortable for older, less flexible paddlers. Most performance-oriented open canoes and some older, large volume C-1's can be paddled with a seat height of 8 inches. The added comfort these extra inches mean for the average person is quite remarkable! If the hull design permits, larger people may want to sit as high as 10 or 12 inches. Note that this will be too high for smaller people to assume a comfortable, balanced kneeling position. If a higher seat makes you feel unstable, lower it until you feels secure.

Bench Seats

Bench seats are found in most general-purpose open canoes. They are made from molded plastic or a wood frame with a woven surface, and hang from the gunwales using metal or wood brackets. Many canoes come from the factory with the seats set too low for a kneeling paddler with large feet to use safely. They must be raised so your feet can slide in and out without becoming snagged underneath. Paddlers who capsize and get caught are subjected to a frightening, occasionally fatal, manhandling. If you plan on paddling whitewater with a bench seat, avoid using bulky footwear like hiking boots. Even when using wetsuit boots, you'll need at least 8 inches of clearance.

Kneeling Thwarts

A kneeling thwart is a flat board hung below the gunwales and angled slightly forward for comfort. It is lighter and less expensive than a bench seat, but you must still consider the need for clearance. Racers like the feel of a thwart; it gives them a true "seat of their pants" feel. But several fatalities and innumerable near misses have resulted from low-hung thwarts! Thwarts also get pretty uncomfortable at

the end of a long day, so pad them with 1/4"
Neoprene or Minicell.

Pedestals and Saddles

Pedestals and saddles are the most popular types of
whitewater canoe seats. Made from thick, soft
Minicell set lengthwise along the keel line, they can
be cut and shaped to fit a paddler exactly. Pedestals

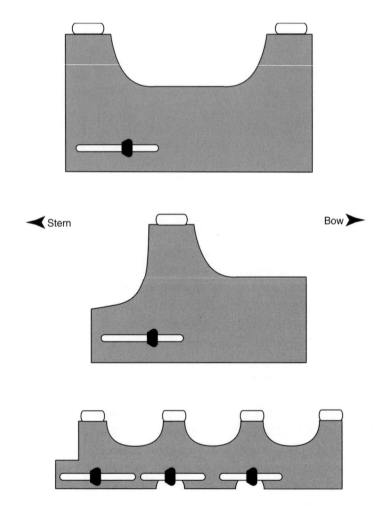

can be freestanding or set under one thwart placed behind the paddler. Saddles use two thwarts, fore and aft. Since there is nothing overhanging your feet, the risk of snagging a foot after capsizing is eliminated.

Pedestals and saddles have a number of advantages. First, attaching the top of your pedestal to a thwart improves its lateral stability. Second, by providing support for the hull below, this setup reduces the amount of inward flex, or oilcanning, that occurs when paddling. It also makes it harder to wrap the boat during a pin. Supported pedestals have an added advantage; they can be installed with inexpensive contact cement rather than a more expensive two-part urethane adhesive.

Thwarts used to install a pedestal are set high off the bottom of the canoe to increase leg clearance and reduce the chance of catching you leg after capsizing. Freestanding pedestals can reduce the risk even further, allowing you to wear thigh straps higher on your upper leg without increasing entanglement risks. The major downside of this setup is that the center thwart must be removed. This weakens the structure of a canoe considerably, making it more vulnerable to pinning and wrapping. Because freestanding pedestals are attached to the canoe only at the bottom, they must be at least 9" wide for stability. Two-part urethane adhesive must be used to strengthen the bond with the hull.

Pedestals and saddles are the most popular types of canoe seats.

Making a Foam Pedestal

Pre-molded pedestals and saddles are available, but these can be expensive. Homemade foam pedestals are an option for budget-minded paddlers with access to a bandsaw and a wholesale supplier of Minicell. Wholesalers can sometimes be found in large cities in the Yellow Pages under "Foam" or "Packing Materials." Minicell typically comes with a thick, smooth "skin" on the outside. Removing this skin with a belt sander or bandsaw before gluing results in tighter, cleaner glued joints.

Minicell is quite expensive, so lay out your proposed design carefully before you start to cut. A water-soluble marker leaves lines that are easily removed later. The sketches on the previous page give a rough outline of both thwart-supported and freestanding saddles. Holes in the three-position saddle allow water to move from side to side to improve your balance when swamped. Once the pieces are cut, the sides of the seat can be rounded with dragon skin until a comfortable profile is achieved.

Locating a Seat Correctly

In open or decked whitewater canoes, seats must be placed so the boat is properly trimmed—that is, balanced evenly fore and aft. Often the manufacturer or a fellow paddler will tell you where to put the seat. If not, take your canoe to calm water and sit inside it, on the pedestal, while a friend watches. Move the seat forward or back as necessary until the bow and stern are at equal heights above the surface. Mark the spot with a water-soluble marker.

This may sound silly, but make sure you know which end of the canoe is the bow! If in doubt, ask the owner, seller, or manufacturer. Some designs are very similar fore and aft. Even with asymmetrical hulls, choosing the correct end is harder than it sounds. Some very experienced people have made this mistake more than once!

Seat positioning for tandem canoeists depends on the paddler's relative weight and whether they paddle in the traditional "end-hole" or the newer "center cockpit" configuration. The latter, with the two paddler's seats roughly 4 feet apart, is popular among serious doubles teams for whitewater. A third seat, for solo trips, can be placed in the middle.

Unless you can get a recommendation from the builder of your boat or a similarly-sized team using the same design, you'll have to find seat locations by trial and error. There are several possible ways to balancing a tandem canoe. For example, if the boat is bow-heavy, one or both paddlers can move their seats towards the stern to trim it.

Decked C-1's are pretty easy to deal with; the cockpit almost always indicates correct seat placement. Decked C-2's can be trickier. When buying fiberglass C-2's, purchase the boat with the cockpit rims uninstalled if you and your partner's weight

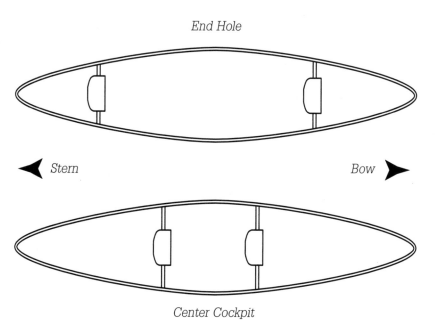

End Hole

Stern   *Bow*

Center Cockpit

differs by more than 10 pounds. Start with small cockpit holes prior to on-water balancing. Once you know where each paddler sits you can widen the openings and install the cockpit rims. It's also common for racing teams to "offset" their seats towards each paddler's strong side for easier paddling. This requires careful balancing and may make the boat difficult to roll.

Once you have the front to back positioning set, be sure that the seat is centered from side to side. A pedestal that is "slightly off" is very annoying to paddle! Measure the distance from the gunwales to the bottom and top of the pedestal, front and back, top and bottom, on both sides. Once you're certain the pedastal is correctly located, outline bottom of the pedestal with a water-soluble marker.

Surface Preparation

To prepare a Royalex hull to bond with a pedestal, knee pads, or D-Rings, wipe it clean with Toluene, a paint thinner available in hardware stores. Rubbing alcohol also works, but avoid gasoline, kerosene, or anything else that leaves a greasy film.

Contact cement requires warm temperatures for a good bond.

With fiberglass boats, sand the hull lightly, through the smooth finish coat and down to the fibers. Any previous outfitting should be sanded smooth, but take care not to cut into the hull.

Polyethylene-based boats are tricker. Nothing sticks to them using normal methods. Both Vinabond and Industrial Adhesive will adhere to a prepared hull, but for best results use Old Town's Discovery Adhesive. Old Town's two-part polyurethane resin is rather expensive, but is highly recommended for skid plates, D-rings, knee pads, and pedestals. To get a good bond, use sandpaper to abrade the

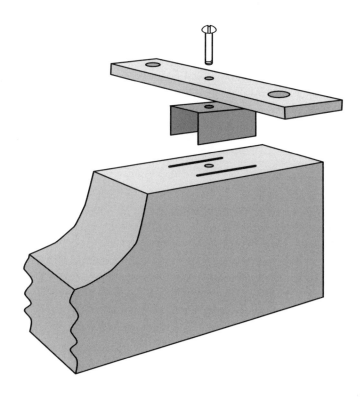

surface thoroughly. Next, set your propane torch to produce a 3 to 4 inch high flame, then pass it across the hull so that the bright blue inner flame touches the entire prepared surface. This changes the polarity of the polyethylene material so glues and resins can grab hold of it. The parts can then be glued in place.

Contact cement requires warm temperatures (at least 60 degrees) and dry air for a good bond. A heat gun or hairdryer can be used to dry the glue in marginal conditions. Apply the glue to both sides of the joint. The glue dries to a tack-free state, where it is still sticky, but will not pull away when touched.

The two sides of the joint are then lined up and pressed together. Once they are touched, they'll grab. You have only one chance to do it right. Practice lining up one edge and lowering the pieces into place before applying the glue. Afterwards, apply firm pressure all across the foam to insure a complete bond.

Hull temperatures must be taken into account. If you bring a canoe into your shop in cold weather, always allow the hull to warm to room temperature before working on it. Otherwise, the glue will not set up correctly.

Seat Installation

Once you have prepared the canoe surface, you are ready to install the seat. Trim saddle or pedestal height flush with the bottom of the thwart. Some people simply glue the top of a foam seat to the underside of the thwart. A stronger installation requires the use of a U-shaped bracket, 1"-2" wide and 3"-4" long, made from galvanized steel or copper sheet. Bolt the bracket to the thwart so that the two ends of the U are sticking down. Ease the thwart down into position: The bracket will leave two marks. Make a stabbing cut on these marks with a sharp-pointed knife roughly as deep as the brackets, then replace the thwart. This time the bracket will bury itself deeply into the foam.

As an alternative, an extra-long bolt can be attached to the thwart. When driven into the pedestal from above it will increase the strength of the installation. Bolt the thwart into place and repeat with the second thwart if a saddle installation is being done.

Free-Standing Pedestals stress the bond between the boat and the seat more than those which are supported by a thwart. The right glue is critical to successful installations: contact cement isn't strong enough, so use a two part urethane adhesive such as 3M's 3532. Good solid contact with the hull is a must for the glue to work. If your canoe's hull profile is V-shaped or rounded it will be necessary to contour the bottom of the pedestal similarly to insure a good, stable placement. This may require the use of a belt sander.

Mix the two-part adhesive and spread it out on the bottom of the pedestal like peanut butter on bread. Tongue depressors or a small body mechanic's squeegee make good applicators. Since pressure forces excess adhesive outward, it should be thick, but not drippy, at the center and thinner on the sides. Carefully line up the front or back of the pedestal with the guide marks, then lower it into place. Place 30-50 pounds of weight on top of the seat for 6-8 hours to hold it tight against the hull until the adhesive hardens.

Knee Pads
and Knee Cups

Knee pads provide comfort and impact protection in whitewater canoes. They can be cut from Minicell or purchased pre-cut from a local outfitter. Wedge-shaped knee pads fit people of various sizes, a good option if several people will use the canoe. These pads are glued to the bottom of the boat with the wide part on the inside, creating a cup for the knees. If the canoe will be used by one person, knee cups are a good idea. Knee cups have semicircular depressions cut into them for a more secure grip. They do require more exact placement. It's usually easiest to make them from several pieces of foam glued together.

Install knee pads after the seat is in place.

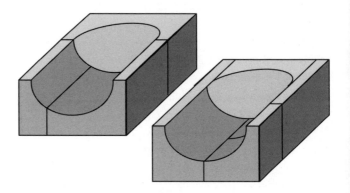

Install knee pads and cups after the seat is in position. Kneel in your canoe with your legs spread comfortably at approximately shoulder width. Place the pads underneath your knees and trace their position with a water-soluble marker. Check to see that the pads are spaced evenly; one should not be set further forward or out to one side than the other. Prepare the surface, and apply contact cement to the knee pads and the point of attachment. Put the pads in place by lining up the top edge with your guiding marks, then lowering them into position. Press firmly, then kneel on them to insure an even bond.

Thigh Straps

Thigh straps, also known as thigh braces, allow you to grab hold of a canoe and maintain a comfortable kneeling position in rough water. They're usually made with 2" wide nylon webbing with buckle or Velcro fasteners, and come both with and without padding. Buckles are a bit harder to adjust, but less likely to release unexpectedly when wet. This is especially important if you roll an open canoe. If Velcro is used, it should be 2" wide and 10" long to hold in wet conditions. You can also make good, cheap thigh straps from used seat belts purchased from an auto junkyard.

Quick-release buckles are designed into some types of thigh straps to allow paddlers to release themselves quickly if necessary. The buckles should be positioned on the upper end of the thigh strap, near the gunwales, so they can be easily reached in an emergency. If you can reach a quick-release buckle set on the keel line, you probably won't need to use it.

Attaching Anchors

Thigh straps are held in place by anchors glued directly to the bottom of the canoe. There are several types. D-Ring anchors are usually sewn to a large, circular patch of vinyl. They are glued into Royalex canoes using Vinabond, a contact cement. Hypalon patches require the use of shore adhesive, also a contact cement. The latter works on both Royalex and Fiberglass boats.

For a mid-thigh installation, four anchors are needed. Two are installed at the center of the boat, roughly 6" apart and 3" to 6" behind the front of the knee. The two side anchors are installed below the gunwale, level with the hipbone. Although one center anchor can be used, two allow a better thigh brace fit and provide a backup in case one blows out. Very large people like the side anchors installed just below the gunwales; smaller paddlers can lower these anchors as much as 8" below the gunwales for a tighter, more secure fit.

To place the anchors, first mark the position of

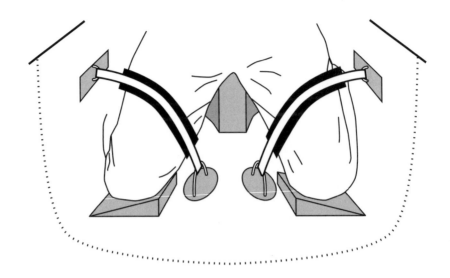

the anchors by tracing them with a water-soluble marker. Prepare the surface as described earlier, apply adhesive to the back of the patch and the hull, and allow it to dry tack-free. Lower the patches into place, then go over the entire surface with a smooth, rounded tool. A metal roller, available from suppliers of raft repair materials, is especially nice.

Anchors made by Pacific Water Sports hold the D-Rings in place with a hard plastic extrusion. They're much smaller than patches and can be made to fit the contours of the boat by submerging them in boiling water for 5 minutes, bending them, then dunking them into cold water to set the shape. Use 3M Urethane Adhesive for installation. After the attachment spots have been marked and prepared, hold the extrusion by its D-Ring and spread the adhesive on the underside, like peanut butter. Set it into place, then place weights on top to hold it securely until it dries. Be careful; the weight may cause the D-Rings to creep on a very slight downslope. Lean the weight up against another heavy object if needed.

If you're not sure what placement works best, experiment by kneeling in your canoe and moving the strap into various positions across your leg. Note where the anchors would need to be to hold the strap in place.

To combine superior boat control and manageable entrapment risks, thigh straps should cross your leg diagonally at mid thigh. This will hold down your entire leg from the knee to the hip without blocking a quick exit. To leave the canoe, pull your knee back, out of the straps, then push it forward. Positioning the strap too farther forward makes it harder to grab hold, even if a paddler is using toe blocks.

Some paddlers prefer their thigh straps to cross their upper leg just below the crotch. This includes canoeists who compete in rodeos (who often combine the high thigh straps with a second pair of knee straps crossing 4-6" behind the knee). High thigh straps feel more secure, especially to smaller paddlers, but users must now pull their legs farther back to get free of the straps, increasing the risk of entanglement. This placement should only be used with free-standing pedestals.

Toe Blocks

Toe blocks allow you to use your feet to push your knees and thighs forward, into the knee cups and thigh straps. Properly positioned, they eliminate the need for over-tightened and restrictive thigh straps. Toe blocks also allow you to pull back out of your straps in easier sections of river, then push forward to tighten up in more serious rapids.

One-Position Toe Blocks

Toe blocks can be nothing more than blocks of foam glued into place. A shaped piece of PVC, like Mad River's "Foote Blocks" can also be used. Most open canoeists like to set them up so their feet curl under and against them when their legs are in position. Others like to lay the top of their foot flat against the hull, with their toes pointed and barely touching the blocks. Either way, they must be positioned exactly or they become quite uncomfortable.

Sit in your canoe with the thigh straps in place and mark the correct position for the blocks. Do this several times to be certain. Although foam installed with contact cement will work for a while, I recommend using 3M Industrial Adhesive for a permanent setup. This is absolutely mandatory when using parts made from ABS plastic.

Adjustable Toe Blocks

Easier to install, adjustable toe blocks can be moved to any paddler perfectly. They are made by attaching adjustable kayak-pedal-style footbraces back-to-back through a foam pedestal. This is most easily done prior to installing a pedestal, but retrofits are possible.

Various installation kits are available, but a length of 1/4" threaded rod works fine. While drilling holes through a foam pedestal is a nice touch, it's much easier and just as effective to simply push the rods through the foam. Be sure to set the rods high enough from the hull so that the footbraces clear the bottom and slides easily. You may need to drill holes in the footpegs to allow the rods to slide through easily, before bolting them tightly into place. A

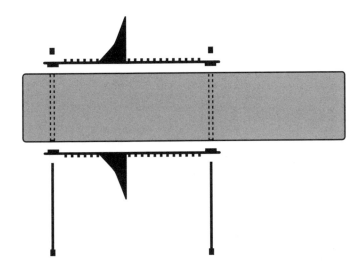

backup plate placed between the footbraces and the Minicell is a nice finishing touch; use a 2-inch-wide strip of ABS plastic or copper.

Some pedestals are too short for footbraces to be positioned correctly. In this case you can glue a second piece of Minicell of the same width behind the pedestal. The back end of the footbrace can now be attached with a threaded rod and nuts. Use 3M Urethane Adhesive to hold the extension securely to the hull.

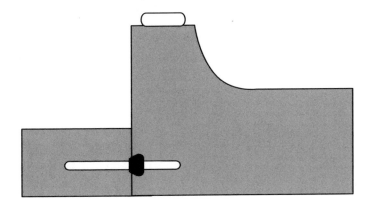

Ankle Blocks

When using toe blocks your feet can get contorted into a variety of uncomfortable positions. Ankle blocks support your feet, lifting ankle joints into a more comfortable alignment. Exactly what works best depends on how each paddler's ankles are constructed, but here are a few ideas. Putting a rounded piece under your ankle raises it up; a wedge-shaped piece coming in from the side also lifts your ankle off the hull. In each case, your bones line up better for less discomfort and fewer circulatory problems. Experiment until you discover the right combination.

Outfitting C-1's

Outfitting a C-1 is very similar to outfitting open canoes, but you must work within the confines of the cockpit. The pedestal is usually no wider than 6 inches, and if thigh braces are to be placed safely, toe blocks are almost essential. The alternative is to tighten the thigh strap until it cuts off circulation, and this makes bailing out difficult. All but the smallest paddlers will need to point their toes, rather than curl them under, when using toe blocks.

Toe blocks are not usually provided in commercially made C-1's. If the bottom of the pedestal is made of ABS plastic, you can drill through it, install the threaded rod, and attach the footbraces. Positioning your knee pads may be complicated by a small cockpit opening and a low deck. Large paddlers with thick legs may have trouble getting their knees wide enough apart. Lastly, be aware that a low rear deck can catch your feet just like a low seat. The clearance afforded by some racing designs may be inadequate for bigger people.

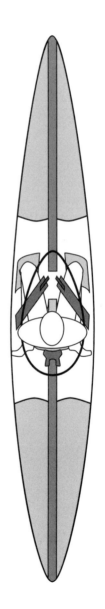

Kayak to C-1 Conversions

Because C-1's are relatively unpopular compared to kayaks nowadays, there are fewer designs available to the avid C-1 paddler. A number of rotomolded kayaks have been converted into C-1's with varying degrees of success. Keep in mind that rotomolded kayak cockpits are narrower than those found on fiberglass C-1's, so these conversions work best for small to mid-sized people. Once you have identified the kayak you wish to convert, here is what you need to do:

- Unbolt and remove the kayak seat.
- Purchase a pedesatal base from Dagger or Perception. Most of the conversions I've seen use a Gyramax pedestal base.
- Pad out the pedestal. Check the position of the pedestal by paddling in flat water, moving the seat fore or aft as needed to trim the boat evenly.
- Bolt the pedestal into position. Use foam to attach the pedestal to the rear wall so the back deck is supported.
- Extend the front wall as needed to secure it to the pedestal. This will keep the wall from falling over.
- Install knee pads.
- Thigh straps should be bolted to the deck at the sides, then attach them to the pedestal at the center. The straps themselves must be shorter than those found in open canoes.
- Adjustable toe blocks can be bolted through the pedestal.

Supporting the Deck

The decks of many C-1's are supported from the inside to maintain their shape and protect the paddler. Although no type of construction or bracing will keep a boat from collapsing under extreme pressure, it should handle routine compression from broaches and enders and provide a few seconds of escape time in more intense situations.

Deck support is usually provided by length-wise "walls," or "pillars." Made from Minicell or some other closed cell foam. They run the entire length of the keel line between the deck and the hull except in the cockpit area. These walls should be 3" wide for stability. They extend into all but the last 6" of the bow and stern, and fit the interior exactly. If fitted carefully they will not collapse or fall over.

The best way to produce a template for walls is to set your boat on its side above a piece of cardboard or wrapping paper. Move a plumb line or builder's square along the edge of the boat, tracing the boat's sideways profile onto the material. Do this twice to catch any errors. Cut the template out, check it for fit,

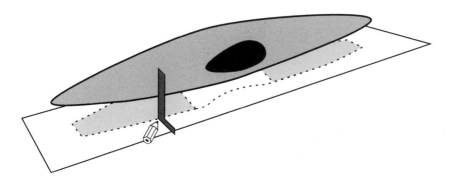

then trace the outline onto a slab of Minicell foam.

Walls are often glued into fiberglass boats, but contact cement is impossible to use in close quarters. Instead, coat the edges of the walls with epoxy resin or Liquid Nails, a paneling adhesive found in hardware stores. The tapered walls will slide into place, positioned, and held until the adhesive dries. Have a cloth handy to wipe up the excess adhesive that is squeezed out.

Because nothing sticks permanently to roto-molded polyethylene hulls, walls in these boats must be attached mechanically. In roto-molded boats, the pedestal assembly is bolted into place, supporting the deck at the sides of the cockpit and anchoring the bottom end of the front and rear walls. Roto-molded or metal brackets, bolted to the underside of the deck, hold the top of the walls in place. The structural integrity of your boat depends on these bolts. They should be checked regularly to see that they are tight. Bolting brackets through the bottom of the boat is not a good idea, as they will inevitably leak after being hit by rocks.

Sprayskirts

Sprayskirts are a critical part of decked boat outfitting. They have a difficult job to do. They must stay in place as boat and paddler are tossed about in huge whitewater, yet release instantly when required. Most are made of neoprene

Undersized sprayskirts will pop-off too easily.

Since C-1 paddlers sit higher in their boats than kayakers, the belly band is worn around the hips, not the waist. An elastic bottom attaches the sprayskirt to the boat. Fiberglass boats have a deep, overhanging cockpit rims that hold sprayskirts extremely well. Cockpit rims on roto-molded boats have more rounded edges and shallower combings that are harder to grip.

Adjustable shock-cord sprayskirts are cheaper to buy, easier to put on, and come off easily when you bail out. They're great for beginning paddlers, but can pop off prematurely in big water. Expert paddlers can't live with an unexpected release in the middle of a Class IV-V drop! The best way to avoid problems is for the sprayskirt to fit the cockpit opening very tightly. These sprayskirts usually won't release less the paddler pulls back on the grab loop, a feat which requires coolness and presence of mind. A paddler who can not locate the loop could become trapped! This prospect is rather intimidating to novices, who should avoid these sprayskirts until properly trained.

A tight fit is not achieved by making a sprayskirt smaller; it should actually fit the opening with very little stretching across the front and some looseness in the sides and back. If your sprayskirt is undersized, it will continually pop off. Instead, the attachment to the cockpit rim is made more secure by adding a thick "rand" made of heavy gum rubber or oversized shock cord to the bottom. The grab loop should be designed to stick out so it cannot be accidently pushed inside the boat. Anyone using a tight-fitting sprayskirt for the first time should practice several wet exits on flat water before getting onto a river.

You can increase your sprayskirt's holding power by roughing up the underside and edges of the cockpit rim with sandpaper or by applying a layer of contact cement to these surfaces. Sprayskirts on larger cockpits also have a tendency to collapse inward due to water pressure. To prevent this, the deck can be designed to fit a bit loosely to absorb the shock. Alternatively, an implosion bar can be sewn in across the front deck. Tight-fitting sprayskirts are most easily attached when wet. If yours is so tight you can't get it on easily, leave it on your boat and for a week or two. This will stretch out the rand and mold the neoprene to the shape of the cockpit.

In Closing

The outfitting techniques described here are designed to increase comfort, improve boat control, and allow quick emergency exits. Remember that you alone are responsible for safety when outfitting your boat. Test all new outfitting carefully before taking it onto moving water. Although this can be done on dry land by experienced boaters, I recommend trying several wet exits in a swimming pool or lake, with help standing bye to eliminate any doubt. If you are having problems exiting the boat while paddling figure out what is causing the trouble and fix it. It may be your only warning.